THE JUNKYARD

By Pat Birtwistle

Illustrations by Bradley Moore
Original Cover Drawing by Antonio Montana Morales

ISBN 0-9733663-4-6

Patnor Publishing

The Junk Yard

By Pat Birtwistle

Cover Illustration By:

Antonio Montana Morales

ACKNOWLEDGMENTS

A heartfelt thanks to Pat Nelson (my friend and research consultant) for her help and encouragement, Nick Sidoti for his enthusiasm, wealth of ideas and insights; Ann Marie Crocco for allowing the students in her school to pilot these novelettes and her encouragement; Angela Marcov who piloted these novelettes and showed such enthusiasm, and to Dot Wishart and Mary Cordeiro for their editing skills. And a special thanks to Paul Dayboll for his help with how to best get these books printed and for creating our website.

Above all, a very special thanks to Norm, my husband and best friend, for all his hard work in making these books become a reality.

The Junk Yard

By Pat Birtwistle

Keep Out!

Chapter 1

There it was again - that dog. Kim stopped. She wanted to run, but her legs would not let her.

"Why?" she was thinking. "Why did I come here? Why didn't I ask the kids to come with me? They would have come if I had asked them."

She wanted to yell for help, but she could not. If she did yell, the dog would find her. Then, the dog ran past her and she could see how big and dirty it was. It did not look up at Kim. Again, Kim kept still. She did not want the dog to find her in its yard.

"I will just stay here and see if the kids will come looking for me. The dog may go and lie down. The man may come back and take the dog into the shop. Then I could make a run for it."

As Kim sat on the top of the hill of junk, her blood was running fast. The wind was cool, but she was so upset that she felt hot.

She was mad at herself for coming here without the rest of the kids. Her folks would be upset, and she did not want that. She was just asking for trouble by coming here.

The dog ran up and down. It had not seen Kim. It had the run of the yard. You could tell that it felt that someone was in the yard. But, it could not find that someone. It had run past Kim, but had not seen her yet. It just kept running by the pile of junk where Kim sat. If it looked up, it would see her.

"Why is it out?" Kim asked herself. "That dog is not out in the day. We have come here a lot. The man keeps the dog with him in the shop all day. So why is it out now?"

Kim had not seen the gate with 'KEEP OUT'. The gate was not open. The man who ran that junk yard kept, 'KEEP OUT', on the gate when he was not there. He would let the dog out, too. That was why the dog had the run of the yard on this day. Kim had come into the yard the back way. She had not come by the gate and that is how she got herself into this mess.

Kim spotted a stool in the junk. She could not see the dog, so she got it and sat down. That was when the dog spotted her and came running over. It came running at her, up the hill of junk to where she was sitting. Kim grabbed junk to pitch at it. That did not stop the dog. It still came at her.

Kim kicked stuff down at the dog. It kept coming at her. She pitched, pushed and kicked a lot of stuff down at the dog. At last, the dog stopped. Then looking up at Kim, it began up the hill again - one step at a time.

"Stop! Go! Get out of here," she yelled at it.

As she was yelling, she was crying. One bit of junk hit the dog. Then, a tool that Kim kicked, hit the dog, and it stopped. The dog made a little cry, but it did not back off. It stayed where it was. Now it was mad! The skin was split where the tool hit. Blood began running down the dog's leg.

When Kim saw that the dog stopped, she stopped pitching stuff. The dog looked up at her and softly said, "Grrrr!"

Then the dog lay down but kept looking up at Kim. She could see blood on the dog's leg where the tool had hit it. Kim felt sad that she had hurt the dog. Kim liked dogs and she would not want to hurt them. But, this dog was after her. She did not want to think of what the dog would do to her if she did not stop it. She had seen the dog before, but now it looked bigger. Kim was thinking that this was the biggest dog she had seen.

As Kim looked down at the dog, she was sobbing, "I did not want to hit you. You are just doing a job. I should not be here. I am the one making the trouble. I should not be here. I just want to get down and get out of here. Will you let me do that? Will you let me get out of here?"

Then she yelled at the dog, "Go! Get out of here! Back off!"

The dog got up. He kept looking up at Kim as the blood ran down its leg. It took one step up to Kim. Then it took one more step. It kept looking at Kim. Kim was sobbing as she got up. She kicked stuff at the dog and kept yelling. "Get back! Get out of here!"

"Grrrr," said the dog as he took one more step.

Chapter 2

"Should we find Kim and Beth and ask them to play too?" Dan asked. "We could get them to play. I bet they would like to play pool."

"They do not like playing pool. You just want them to play so you can win. You cannot win playing us, so you want the girls to play," Bob said.

"Will you stop it?" said Nick. "It's just pool. You two are too much! Let's not make a big thing of it. We're just going to have some fun. Come on!"

"Trouble! Trouble! Trouble!" Dan said. "We just can't seem to stay out of trouble. It is not as if we look for it."

"But," said Nick, "we did go to the swamp and the old house. If we had stayed out of there, we would not have had trouble. It is up to us to stay away from spots like that. Our folks did tell us not to go out there. So, in a way, we do look for trouble."

Bob said, "Well, let's just play some pool. We can't get into trouble doing that." So, off they went to play pool at Bob's house.

Beth was sitting at her house. She could not think of what to do for the day. She just sat on the steps looking at a little bag playing in the wind. The wind would flip the bag and push it up, then let the bag down a little, then flip it up and down. The bag landed.

"I want to have some fun," Beth was thinking. "This is no fun. I do not like playing pool, so I can't do that. Kim likes to do stuff. She is not playing pool with the kids, so she and I could do something. Kim can think of a lot of things that are fun. She could be doing something that I could do with her. I'll find her and see what she is up to."

Beth jumped up and took off for Kim's house. On the way, she was trying to think of ways that they could have some fun. When she got to Kim's, there was no one there. Sometimes Kim's Mom took Kim to the lake to go swimming. So, Beth sat on the steps. Kim and her Mom did not stay at the lake after they had a swim. "They will be back soon," Beth was thinking.

Then Beth saw Kim's Mom coming down the block. Kim was not with her. She had some bags and looked as if she could use a hand. So Beth went to help her.

"Hi, Beth! What are you doing here?" Kim's Mom asked.

"I came to see if Kim wanted to do something," Beth said, as she took some of the bags. Beth liked Kim's Mom. She was one of the moms that were good to the kids. She didn't get too upset when the kids got into trouble.

"Some of the kids are playing pool over at Bob's house. Kim and I do not like to play pool. So, I was thinking we could find something to do. She is good at the thinking up things to do. Where is she?" asked Beth.

"Kim is not here," her mom said. "She left before I went to get this stuff. I can't think of where she would go if she is not with you or the rest of the kids."

They went up the steps and Kim's mom pushed the door open. She put the bags down and went to get some water. "Do you want some water, Beth?" she asked.

"No, I'm OK," Beth said.

She was looking at Beth with an odd look. "Why is she look ng at me like that?" Beth was thinking.

Then, Kim's mom said, "Kim is trying to get rich. She gets into trouble when she is thinking of ways to get rich. Do you think she is up to something?"

Beth did not want to think that Kim could be in trouble. They were in too much trouble.

All the kids had said they would stay out of trouble. Beth looked at Kim's mom and could tell that she was upset.

"Look," said Beth. "Kim would not find trouble if she was not with someone. She would not do something that would upset you. We all made a pact to keep out of trouble. I will look for her. Do not get upset. I will find her. It will be OK. I think she will be at the rock by the swamp. That is where she likes to go when she is by herself." Beth didn't want Kim's mom to be upset, but Beth could not think of where Kim could be.

As Beth left Kim's house she was thinking, "Kim, where are you? What are you doing? Where should I look for you? Why didn't you come to get me when you left?"

Beth felt that Kim was in trouble but, she didn't want to let on to Kim's Mom. She could not think of where to look for Kim. She would have to look in all the spots that kids went to. There were not a lot of spots where the kids hung out. So, Beth had to find somewhere that Kim liked to go when she was not with the rest of the kids. "The big rock by the swamp is a good spot. That is where a lot of the kids hang out. She must be there," Beth said to herself.

Chapter 3

"Grrrr," the dog kept coming at Kim. There was nowhere she could go. If she ran, the dog would be on her before she could get down the hill of junk. Kim looked past the dog. She was looking for a way out. She could not see one. She was thinking fast.

"If I make a run for it, I will not make it. They say, 'Do not run if the dog is mad or upset.' That just makes the dog get more upset. So I can't run! I could just keep pitching stuff at it, but that does not seem to stop this dog. It just keeps coming at me. Yelling at it will not help at all. Maybe I can make it stay back if I say things softly to the dog. I think that may do it!"

So, Kim said softly, "It's OK, boy. You lay down. I will not throw more stuff at you. You are just doing the job that the boss wants you to do. It's OK. Just let me get out of here. Good boy. Just lay down. See, I am just going to sit down and let you rest. Good boy. That's it."

The dog stopped. It was as if it liked the way Kim said things softly. It began a little crying and lay down. Kim kept saying softly, "Will you let me out of here? I will not take stuff if you just let me go. Good boy! You just stay there. Good boy!"

The dog was looking up at her as she began to back away from it. The dog lay still but kept looking at Kim as she got up and took a step up. The dog got up. Kim would step back. Then the dog would step up the hill at her. Kim tripped on some junk and fell. She landed but pushed herself up and began yelling at the dog again. That spooked the dog and it came at her.

She grabbed as much stuff as she could lay her hands on and kept pitching it at the dog as she was yelling. All this did not stop the dog. Soon, he was coming at her a little faster. It did not stop looking at Kim. Kim kept backing up, but she kept tripping over junk because she could not look away from the dog. She still wanted to run, but cou d not. She could not think of a good plan, so she just kept backing up.

The dog wanted this girl to do something. He wanted her to run. He could go after her and pin her down. Then he could do his job. Why was she saying things softly, then yelling and pitching stuff at him? Did she want to play? He was not here to play.

This was his yard, and he was here to stop kids from coming here. That was what the boss wanted him to do. This girl had come into the yard when the boss was away. No one was to be in the yard then.

The dog's "Grrrr" was not said softly now. He was getting mad because stuff was coming at him. His leg had blood that was dripping, and he wanted to lie down and lick it. But, he had a job to do. He was not going to let this one get away. He would stop her from getting out of the junk yard. "Just let her run and she will find out what I can do," the dog was thinking.

Kim got to the top of the junk and was making her way down the hill now. She was not yet where she could make a run for it.

She could not pitch this stuff too well because the dog was over her. She wanted to rest, but could not because the dog would be on her if she stopped. She had to keep her cool and try to get down the hill little by little. Kim stepped back and grabbed something to pitch at the dog. That is when she fell and went all the way down the hill. When she landed, she hit something and blacked out. The dog saw her go down, jumped over some stuff and ran down the hill as fast as it could go.

"Now I can do my job," it was thinking. "I'll get her." When it got up to Kim, it stopped. It was standing looking down at her. She did not get up. The dog jumped at her.

Chapter 4

"That was so much fun," Bob said. "It was fun because I'm the best."

"You get to play when you want. We just get to play when you ask us to come over," Dan said. He liked to win, too. "So, that's why you are the best. I would be the best if I played all the time."

"Cut it out you two. I don't think I'll play pool with you again. You have to win. What about just playing for fun?" asked Nick.

Bob said, "OK, OK, but I'm still the best!"

They saw Beth coming down the block. She had an odd look. She was not with Kim, so they felt bad that they had not asked her to play pool with them. As she came up to them, she looked more and more upset.

"What's up?" Bob asked.

"Kim is not with you?" she asked.

"Kim does not like to play pool. Why would she be with us? You two do something when we play pool. Where is she? Why would you think that she was with us?"

"That's just it," said Beth. "She is not at her house, and her mom thinks she may be getting into trouble again. I have looked for her at the rock by the swamp and all the spots that I can think of. I cannot find her and cannot think of where she could be."

"Oh, no!" all the boys said.

"Not again," said Nick. "We cannot get into trouble again. Our folks will kill us. We have to find her, or we will all get it."

"Where do you think she would go by herself? She would not go swimming without us. Where would she go by herself?" asked Bob.

"I can't think of one more thing. That's why I came looking for you," said Beth. "What are we going to do?"

"OK, let's do this," said Bob. "Beth, tell us where you have looked for her. Then we'll think about some more spots where she could be. Two of us can go to one spot. It will be faster if we split up."

"But, I went to all the spots that I could think of. I could not think of where she would go when she was not at those spots. Can you?" asked Beth.

They did come up with some more spots to look. Beth went with Bob one way, and Dan went with Nick.

"She would not go into the swamp without us would she?" asked Dan.

"No," Nick said. "She would not do that."

They said that after they looked for her, they would all go to Beth's house. They did not want to go to Kim's because her mom would be too upset. They looked in all the spots where they hung out. No one had seen her. By now, the kids were getting upset, too. It was not like Kim to go off without one of them. It was not like her to be away all day like this.

Not one of the kids they met had seen Kim. That was odd.

When they got to Beth's house, they felt lost. They did not want to tell their folks, but they could not think of what to do.

"Think," said Bob. "Where would Kim go by herself? What would she be up to? She has to be somewhere! Why has no one seen her?"

"Her mom was upset because she said Kim wanted to get rich. She said that Kim kept getting into trouble because she kept looking for a way to be rich. Now, where would she go to look for riches?" asked Beth.

That was when it hit Dan. "When I was with her last," he said, "she said that she had seen on TV that there were lots of things at the junk yard that you could find that were not junk. Sometimes folks pitch things out that they think is junk, but it is not. I'll bet that is where Kim went. Let's go out to the junk yard."

Bob said, "Kim would not go to the junk yard by herself. There are rats at the junk yard. She would not go if we were not with her."

"I think that she would." said Beth. "It is the one spot where we have not looked. No one has seen her, so she must be somewhere like that."

"Let's go!" Dan said.

They all took off for the junk yard. But, would they get there before the dog did something to Kim?

Chapter 5

The dog came up to Kim. It wanted to kill her. It was like a "mad dog" because Kim was in its yard. She should not be here. The dog was hurt, and she did it to him.

"Kill! Kill! Kill!" the dog was thinking.

The dog grabbed Kim's leg. When it did that, Kim lay still and did not cry out. She did not yell or pitch things. That was making the dog more upset. He grabbed her hand, and blood began running down it.

Again, Kim lay still and did not cry out. The dog let the hand go. It gave Kim a push. The skin on her hand had blood all over it now.

*   *   *

The kids were running as fast as they could go to get to the junk yard. They were all thinking that Kim must be in big trouble, or she would be back by now. They could help her if they could find her. But where could she be? That junk yard was big. If she were there at all, it would be a job finding her.

The man that ran the junk yard did not let kids go into the yard. He said that a junk yard was not a spot for them to be. He let all the kids think that he did not like them, and when they came out to the yard, he would yell at them.

"Oh! No!" Nick said as he ran to the yard. "KEEP OUT is on the gate. That is there when the man who runs the yard is not here. He lets the dog out, too. The dog must be in the yard. We can't go in there if that dog is out. Have you seen it? It would kill us if we went in there. Now, what do we do?"

"I could get over the gate, but what do we do if that dog is in there?" asked Dan.

"Kim would not go in there if "KEEP OUT" was on the gate. She has seen that dog and she would not go into the yard. We can go back to Beth's house and see if we can think of where she is," Bob said.

"Kim!" Dan yelled.

"Kim!" they all yelled. But, Kim did not yell back.

The kids could not come up with a plan to get into the yard, and they wanted to get out of there before the man came back. They began going down the hill, but the man came over to the yard and saw them.

"What do you kids want?" he asked.

"Did you look at the gate? Did you see 'KEEP OUT' on it? This is not where kids should be. Did your folks say it was OK for you to come here?" He was mad.

The kids kept still. One of them would have to say something. No one wanted to tell him that they were looking for Kim. They did not want him to start yelling at them. But, they could not think of what to do.

At last Nick said, "We are looking for Kim. We were thinking she may have come to the junk yard looking for stuff that could make her rich. We did not go into the yard when we saw that the gate was not open. But, we think she may be in there. No one has seen her all day, and this is the last spot we could think of to look for her."

"Would you take a look in the yard for her?" asked Beth. "Her mom is upset and so are we. We think that she could be in trouble."

"Kids!" The man said.

He looked over at the yard. The dog had not run out to the gate. It was not like the dog not to come to the gate when the man came back. He yelled for the dog. The dog still did not come out of the yard. The man went to the gate and opened it. He went into the yard and shut the gate. He did not look back at the kids. He went to the back of the yard. A little way back he saw the dog. It was licking something.

The man made his way over the junk to have a look. The dog was licking Kim's hand. As the man came over, the dog looked up at him.

By now Kim had come to. She lay still so the dog would not hurt her. She looked up at the man, but she did not get up. The man helped her. He was cross, but he had a soft spot for kids. He did not want them in the yard because they could get hurt.

"Some kids are looking for you, girl" he said. "We should get you out of here."

Kim took a step or two and then had to rest. The man helped her back to the gate. When the kids saw her, they did not say a thing. They wanted to get her back to Beth's before her mom came looking for her.

As they went past the man, he yelled at them. "Do not come back here again. You will be in big trouble if I find you here!"

"Grrrr," said the dog.

New Start Suspense Series - Part 1

The Swamp
The Old House
What A Day
The Junk Yard
The Trip
At The Mall
The Junk Yard

Kim wants to be rich. One day she goes to the junk yard to look for stuff that could make her rich. Things get bad for her when she gets trapped. No one can find her. The kids do not want Kim's mom to find out that she is lost. They look in all the spots that they can think of, but still no Kim. At last, Dan says that they should go to the junk yard. When they get there the gate is shut and has "Keep Out" on it.

"I really liked reading this book."
Phillippe

www.ingramcontent.com/pod-product-compliance
Lightning Source LLC
Chambersburg PA
CBHW060648030426
42337CB00018B/3507